WG

The Book of
Florida Wisdom

The Book of Florida Wisdom

Common Sense and Uncommon Genius From 101 Floridians

Compiled and Edited by Criswell Freeman

WALNUT GROVE PRESS
P.O. Box 58128
Nashville, TN 37205
(615) 256-8584

ISBN 0-9640955-9-9

WALNUT GROVE PRESS books are available at special discounts for sales in bulk purchases, fund-raising, or educational use. For information, contact WALNUT GROVE PRESS.

Printed in the United States of America
by Vaughan Printing, Inc.
Book Design by Armour&Armour
Cover Design by Mary Mazer
Typesetting & Page Layout by Sue Gerdes
Proofreading by Words, Word, Words
1 2 3 4 5 6 7 8 9 10 • 95 96 97 98

ACKNOWLEDGMENTS
The author gratefully acknowledges the helpful support of Mary Ann Cleveland, Mary Susan Freeman, Don Pippen, Margaret Queen, Cindy Wise and all the writers who have chronicled the history and wisdom of Florida.

To The Memory of

Mamie T. Willoughby

Table of Contents

Introduction

Florida is not a single place; it is many places. It is, at once, very old and very new. It is a place of passing through and a place of settling down. It is as cosmopolitan as Miami, as easygoing as the Panhandle, and as wild as the Everglades. From this diversity springs a wisdom that is unique to the Sunshine State.

This book is a treasury of sound advice from 101 Floridians. Not all of these men and women are natives. Edison, for example, owned a winter home in Fort Meyers but also maintained his New Jersey residence. Ernest Hemingway, a native of Illinois, was a fixture of Key West. And Walt Disney, while not technically a resident of the state, qualifies as an honorary citizen based upon the staggering impact of his Magic Kingdom.

As I conducted the research for this book, I came to an interesting conclusion: Florida is bigger than we think. It is more than tourism, it is more than industry, it is more than the wild beauty of nature or the gleaming steel of skyscrapers. Florida is an assortment of cultures, economies and ecosystems. It stretches from the tropics to Georgia, from the sandy beaches to the Everglades, from sophisticated cities to farms, ranches and groves.

Despite the diversity of its people, the wisdom in this text does share a common thread. It reflects the sunny disposition that logically accompanies life in the king-sized garden called Florida.

1

Florida

To be so new, Florida is a very old place. The land of beachfront skyscrapers and Magic Kingdoms was discovered almost 500 years ago by a misguided Spaniard searching for the Fountain of Youth. Since a day in 1513 when Juan Ponce de León landed near St. Augustine, Florida has been a land in transition. It remains so today.

Florida is like a perennial teenager, always in the process of growing up. First a Spanish territory, she was sold to America in 1819. But America was not sure what to do with her. There were Indian battles, a Civil War, a string of booms and busts. Finally, with the advent of railroads, pesticides, air conditioning and better highways, the Sunshine State assumed its rightful position as the nation's playground.

Marjory Stoneman Douglas once called Florida "the most recognizable feature on the map of the United States of North America." But there is more than shape that distinguishes the land that Ponce de León named after its beautiful flowers. Florida is easily recognizable because everyone, it seems, is planning to go there. With good reason.

We Floridians live in an earthly paradise.

Fuller Warren

Florida does beguile and gratify.

Henry James

As I went farther and farther north and
it got colder and colder, I could see why
Florida is a golden word. The very name of
Florida carried the message of warmth and
ease and comfort. It was irresistible.

John Steinbeck

Florida Wisdom

Florida is for amazement, wonder and delight,
and for refreshment of the soul.

Ernest Lyons

I came to Florida when I was about five years
old, and I always felt cheated
that I wasn't born here.

Burt Reynolds

The charm of Florida cannot be put on paper.
Once felt, however, it lingers with
its victim so long as he draws breath.

Perry and Stockbridge

Florida

There is only one way to know Florida.
That is to live there.
Perry and Stockbridge

The seasons do change in South Florida —
but you have to live there quite
a while to recognize just how.
Ernest Lyons

Here in Florida, the seasons move in and
out like nuns in soft clothing, making
no rustle in their passing.
Marjorie Kinnan Rawlings

Somehow, "autumn" does not seem
properly used in Florida.
Marjorie Kinnan Rawlings

Florida is a very healing place.

Burt Reynolds

Florida, like a piece of embroidery, has
two sides to it — one side all tag-rag and
thumbs, without order or position; and
the other side always showing flowers and
arabesques and brilliant coloring. There is a
right side and a wrong side to everything.

Harriet Beecher Stowe

If I had my say, I wouldn't come north at all.
I leave Florida with tears in my eyes.

Harriet Beecher Stowe

Politically and socially, Florida has its
North and South, but its northern area is
strictly southern and its southern area
definitely northern.

Federal Writer's Project, 1939

The Florida cracker's wants are simple —
his garden plot, pigpen, chicken coop,
and the surrounding woods and streams
that supply him and his family with
nearly all the living necessities.

Federal Writer's Project, 1939

There are no other Everglades in the world. They are, they have always been, one of the unique regions of the earth, remote, never wholly known. Nothing anywhere else is like them! They are unique in the simplicity, the diversity, and the related harmony of the forms of life they enclose.

Marjory Stoneman Douglas

Wild places have always haunted me. Yet I had not anticipated any lure of the Everglades. I was powerfully impressed by this strange region.

Zane Grey

The Everglades is a land of water and rocks, of endless saw grass prairies interspersed with tropical forests, of exquisite snowy egrets and ancient bellowing alligators.

Jack Rudloe

Florida Wisdom

Florida possesses a coast line of about
     twelve hundred miles, of which the larger
half is washed by the Gulf of Mexico. There
seems to be literally no end to the oysters,
     the fish, the sea-birds, the shells, or the
     turtles along these waters; and the shore
and islands abound in the bear, deer, turkey,
opossum and raccoon, and in smaller game.
Sidney Lanier, 1876

In its calmness, its unhurried gait of
     Southern spirit, West Florida is a long way in
mind and in geography from the travel agency
     brochure perception of newer Florida.
Jesse Earl Bowden

Key West is like something seen in a dream.
John Dos Passos

I love Key West. There are a lot of
          incredible characters down there,
     as migratory and gypsy-souled as I am.
Jimmy Buffett

Whaen we pulled into the mustard-yellow
railway station of Miami, we felt
we were in fairyland.

David Fairchild, 1912

In 1912, the most practical way to reach the
West Coast from Miami was via Key West.

David Fairchild

With more than half its nearly two million
people Hispanic in origin, it's no wonder
Miami is called the capital of Latin America.

Fodor's Travel Guidebook

Miami is closer to Havana than to Tallahassee.

David Rieff

Jacksonville and St. Augustine are two cities not fifty miles apart; but the difference between them is just the distance from the nineteenth century to the sixteenth. The former strikes you with all the vim of Andrew Jackson, after whom it is called. In the latter you cannot fail to find a flavor of saintly contemplation which seems to breathe from out the ancient name of the good old father whom Menéndez selected for its patron saint.

Sidney Lanier, 1876

Wealth has its privileges.
That's the continuing reality of Palm Beach.

Fodor's Travel Guidebook

We Floridians are not just "tooting our horn"
when we say that no other state
offers as many opportunities
to encounter gigantic insects.

Dave Barry

Florida is the greatest country in America.

Bill Peterson

2

Florida History

Florida history before Columbus is not wholly clear. We do know of the existence of several dozen Native American tribes; vast numbers of these natives died from European diseases and warfare.

Attempts at permanent European colonization failed until 1565 when the Spaniard Pedro Menéndez de Aviles established St. Augustine. For two centuries, Spain and England struggled for control of the territory; finally, Spain sold Florida to the United States.

The early 1800's were marked by Indian Wars, statehood (in 1845) and the Civil War. In the late 1800's, Henry Flagler and other notable financiers built railroads and hotels that made Florida a viable vacation destination.

The last hundred years has been marked by fantastic growth and periodic retrenchment, but the overall trend remains clear: flowering progress.

All these birds, insects, animals, reptiles,
whispering, screaming, howling, croaking,
fish in their kinds teeming, plants thrusting
and struggling, life in its millions, its billion
forms, the greatest concentration
of living things on this continent,
they made up the first Florida.

Marjory Stoneman Douglas

Here are no lofty peaks seeking the sky,
no mighty glaciers or rushing streams. Here is
land, tranquil in its beauty, serving not as the
source of water but as the last receiver of it.

Harry S Truman
Dedicating the Everglades National Park

Among my services,
I discovered, of my
own cost and charge,
the island of Florida and
others in its district which
are not mentioned as being
small and useless.

Ponce de León in a Letter to Charles V

Pedro Menéndez de Aviles was the real
founder of Florida. The coming of this
practical city builder marked the end of
wandering in search of Eldorado and the
beginning of settlements and trade.

Claude Pepper

I turned and saw a bay, the best that I
have seen in my life — the bay the Indians
call *Pansacola*.

Captain Juan Jordan
Member of the Party that "Rediscovered" Pensacola Bay

The native population of Florida at the time
of the Spanish conquest comprised
approximately 10,000 Indians.

Federal Writer's Project, 1939

Florida Wisdom

We shall fight till the last drop of
Seminole blood has moistened
the dust of our hunting ground.

Osceola

I had rather be killed by a white man in
Florida than die as an old man in Arkansas.

Cooacoochee

There is no truth to saying that you become
a Florida Cracker after getting sand in your
shoes. Not even being born in Florida since
1900 is enough. Your dyed-in-the-wool
genuine Florida Cracker traces his family
back to the Indian Wars.

Ernest Lyons

In the interior of Southern Florida, in and
about what is known as the Everglades,
dwell some three or four hundred Indians —
all that is left in the State of the once
powerful tribe of Seminoles.

Charles B. Cory, 1896

Before the coming of the railroads,
transportation in Florida depended
chiefly on streams and coastal waters.
Overland travel presented a dreary and
discouraging prospect.

Federal Writer's Project, 1939

Mrs. Tuttle, I own the railroad as
completely as I own this cigar or my umbrella.
You have no cause to worry.
The railroad will come to this spot.

Henry Flagler

Prophetic Words Spoken to Miami's Julia Tuttle

With the technical know-how of American
Industry and the creative imagination of the
Disney organization, I'm confident we can
build a living showcase that more people
will talk about and come to look at than
any other area in the world.

Walt Disney

I want a location where I can put everything.

Walt Disney
Describing His Vast Purchase of Land Near Orlando

I believe that this nation should commit
itself to achieve the goal, before the
decade is out, of landing a man on the moon
and returning him safely to Earth.
It will not be one man going to the moon,
it will be an entire nation.

John F. Kennedy, 1961

Florida is at once the oldest and the newest state in the Union.

Ralph Henry Barbour, 1926

3

Advice

For over a century, Floridians have rolled out the welcome mat to visitors from all over the world. In Florida, hospitality is not just a behavior, it's an industry.

Any good host may be called upon for some friendly advice. The best counsel is offered freely, but without demands or pressures. In that spirit, the following words are presented for your consideration. Enjoy these simple suggestions from the Sunshine State.

Do things, not that you may be rich, but that you may be useful.

Henry Flagler

Steadfastly refuse to upset yourself
over something you can't control.

Jim Walter

It isn't that complicated.
Keep it simple, and do a good job.

Wayne Huizenga

My father taught me this:
Do the right thing, never forget your roots,
and always count your blessings.

Shaquille O'Neal

Don't wait for something outside yourself
to make you happy in the future.
Be happy now.

Earl Nightingale

Advice

You can learn or do anything you want
if you aren't hurried.

Jane Wood Reno

Wisdom comes at sixty, not before.

Henry Ward Beecher's Advice to Edward Bok

If you keep thinking what you've always
thought, you'll keep getting
what you've always got.

Wally "Famous" Amos

Absorb ideas from every source.

Thomas Edison

Tradition is very often an excuse word for
people who don't want to change.

Red Barber

Know your strengths and
take advantage of them.

Greg Norman

Make the world a bit more beautiful and
better because you have lived there.

Grandmother's advice to Edward Bok

Don't allow the future to scare you.

Tennessee Williams

Don't be too proud to take lessons. I'm not.

Jack Nicklaus

Don't go where the path may lead.
Go where there is no path and
leave your own trail.

Wally "Famous" Amos

Don't find a fault, find a remedy.

Henry Ford

Florida Wisdom

Don't burn your bridges at both ends.

Bill Peterson

Always be in a state
of becoming.

Walt Disney

Have a code to live by, and live by it.

Jack Knight

Do a worthy service to both God and man.

Claude Pepper

You must pay the price if you wish
to secure the blessing.

Andrew Jackson

In God we trust.

State Motto

Advice

My advice to young people? Do not trust
luck, but be, in every way, as fully prepared
as possible to measure up to the
"lucky breaks" when they come.

James Weldon Johnson

Luck is a crook who ultimately
destroys all those who are taken in by her.
Distinguish between luck and opportunity.

J. C. Penney

People are not remembered by how few times
they fail, but by how often they succeed.
Every wrong step is another step forward.

Thomas Edison

Every time the light turns green,
stay in the thick of competition.

Don Garlits

My advice to kids?
Don't be like me — be better than me.

Shaquille O'Neal

4

Life

Daytona educator Mary McLeod Bethune was asked to give her thoughts on life. She responded simply, "Life is wonderful." In three words, Bethune summed up life in general, and Florida living in particular.

Each day, take a fresh hold on life.

James Weldon Johnson

There are no shortcuts in life.

Don Shula

Any person who passes up the passion of
his times and doesn't become involved,
does so at the cost of not having lived.

LeRoy Collins

My philosophy of life is exceedingly simple:
be fair to everyone; do as much good as you
can; be honest with yourself, which means
honest with everybody.

A. I. du Pont

Time is really the only capital that
   any human being has and the only thing
      he can't afford to lose.

Thomas Edison

Time is the least thing we have.

Ernest Hemingway

It is important to stay close enough
   to the pulse of life to feel its rhythm,
to be comforted by its steadiness, to know
that life is vital, and one's own minute living
   a torn fragment of the larger cloth.

Marjorie Kinnan Rawlings

Life is an unanswered question,
   but let's still believe in the dignity and
      importance of the question.

Tennessee Williams

Middle age is when everything happens.

Marjory Stoneman Douglas

Life is like a bicycle: you don't fall off
unless you stop pedaling

Claude Pepper

Old age is comparative. I don't see
and I don't hear, but those things
can happen at any age.

Marjory Stoneman Douglas
On Her Hundredth Birthday

The grass is greenest right where you are.

Wally "Famous" Amos

Florida Wisdom

It is a wonderful inner personal satisfaction
to reach the point when a man can say:
"I have enough." He feels, for the first time
what a priceless possession is the thing
he never had before: freedom.

Edward Bok

It is more important to live the life one
wishes to live, and to go down with it if
necessary, quite contentedly, than live
more profitably but less happily.

Marjorie Kinnan Rawlings

The greatest waste of money is to keep it.

Jackie Gleason

Americans live to work,
but Cubans work to live.

Cuban Folk Saying

It is always bewildering to change
one's complete way of life.
Marjorie Kinnan Rawlings

Life changes. You better change with it.
John Duda

My father constantly impressed upon me
that nothing in the world possessing life
and animation was easy to imitate.
John James Audubon

Every living thing changes all the time.
David Fairchild

Nothing stands still in this world.
Things get better or worse, bigger or smaller.
It's better to build something instead
of tearing something down.
Bill France

Life and economics, as well as health,
run in cycles, so we must be able
to handle the bitter with the sweet.
J. E. Davis

The unalterable law of life is "grow" or "go."
George and Jane Dusenbury

Don't go to your grave with a life unused.
Bobby Bowden

Discover the talent that God has given you.
Then, go out and make the most of it.
Steve Spurrier

5

Hope

For 500 years, Florida has been a magnet for optimists, dreamers, and visionaries. It was discovered by explorers searching for cities of gold and fountains of youth. It was built by hopeful developers who often risked everything in the process. Disney chose Orlando as the site for his dream factory, while Cape Kennedy served as the launching pad for the dreams of a nation.

Florida is a state built on hope.

Hope

If you can dream it, you can do it.

Walt Disney

Dreams, if they're any good at all,
          are always a little crazy.

Ray Charles

Keep your eyes on your dreams.

Wally "Famous" Amos

Without faith, nothing is possible. With it, nothing is impossible.

Mary McLeod Bethune

Hope

You are what you think you are,
in golf and in life.

Raymond Floyd

Whether you think you can or
think you can't, you're right.

Henry Ford

Human thoughts have the tendency to turn
themselves into their physical equivalents.

Earl Nightingale

For every far-seeing pioneer who has thus
far carved his monument and his fortune
from the soil of Florida, there are a thousand
equal or greater opportunities still open for
men of vision, initiative and courage.

Stockbridge and Perry

We need visions for larger things, for the
unfolding and reviewing of worthwhile things.

Mary McLeod Bethune

My message to you is this:
Be courageous. Have faith. Go forward!

Thomas Edison

Faith in God is the greatest power,
   but great faith too is faith in oneself.

Mary McLeod Bethune

An inquiring mind in which there can be
no room for fear is one of the most precious
   bestowals upon a human being.

Edward Bok

There is a place in God's sun for the youth
   "farthest down" who has the vision, the
determination, and the courage to reach it.

Mary McLeod Bethune

Fear strikes out.

Pete Rose

All our dreams can come true — if we have the courage to pursue them.

Walt Disney

6

Action

Most Americans know Andrew Jackson as the seventh president of the United States, but he also played an important role in the history of Florida. Jackson was called "Old Hickory" for his toughness; as a soldier and Indian fighter, he proved himself worthy of the name. During his tenure as military governor of the Territory of Florida, he often clashed with civilian authorities. Nowhere is it recorded that Jackson ever backed down.

It is said that some men are often in error but never in doubt; Andrew Jackson was a charter member of this fraternity. His advice was straightforward: "Take time to deliberate; but when the time for action arrives, stop thinking and go on."

If you're plagued by procrastination or doubt, consider the following thoughts. They are offered by Floridians who share Old Hickory's penchant for action.

If you know you are right about something,
go after it even if you don't think you can win.
You might be surprised.

LeRoy Collins

You can't build a reputation on
what you're going to do.

Henry Ford

Our greatest weakness lies in giving up.

Thomas Edison

When I make up my mind, I act. If I speak, I will do what I say. If the hail rattles, let the flowers be crushed.

Osceola

Keeping busy is the answer.

Marjory Stoneman Douglas
On Her Hundredth Birthday

Success means hustling all the time, win
or lose. Be aggressive and above all, hustle.

Ron Fraser

Be moral, be ethical, work hard, and
don't pay too much attention to the critics.

Nick Bollettieri

God doesn't want your ability.
He wants your availability.

Bobby Bowden

Nothing counts so much
as character, and
nothing succeeds like
action born in truth.

Edward Bok

Never mistake motion for action.

Ernest Hemingway

I am long on ideas but short on time.
I expect to live to be only about a hundred.

Thomas Edison

It is better to have faith in a cause that will
ultimately succeed than to succeed
in a cause that will ultimately fail.

Bobby Bowden

Never take counsel
of your fears.

Andrew Jackson

7

Other People

Two thousand years ago, the Latin writer Publilius Syrus made a profoundly simple observation about the treatment of others. He warned, "Expect to be treated by others as you have treated them."

Florida is not normally considered a land of conflict, but 500 years ago, this was not the case. The territory was discovered and conquered by Europeans who ignored the advice of Publilius. Centuries of strife ensued.

Today, the Sunshine State is renowned for its hospitality. The following insights will help you earn better treatment from your fellows. You'll earn appreciation and respect the old-fashioned way — by treating others as you would wish to be treated.

The bitterest tears shed over graves are for words left unsaid and deeds left undone.

Harriet Beecher Stowe

Love is a multiplication.

Marjory Stoneman Douglas

Be big enough to serve other people.

Claude Pepper

There's no such thing as a self-made man.

Red Barber

Coming together is a beginning.
Keeping together is progress.
Working together is success.

Henry Ford

Think in terms of what you want to do — the
things you want to accomplish, the ways
you can be of sound benefit.

LeRoy Collins

Life is more than making money, and the
man who misses this truth misses the
greatest joy and satisfaction that can come
into his life — service to others.

Edward Bok

Have faith in God, faith in yourself,
and a desire to serve.

Mary McLeod Bethune

Never lose your zeal for
　　　　building a better world.
Mary McLeod Bethune

Hatred is like acid. It does more damage
　　to the vessel in which it is stored than it
　　can to the object on which it is poured.
Wally "Famous" Amos

Being distracted by the color of a person's
　　skin is something I just can't see.
Ray Charles

I meet discrimination with great pity
in my heart for those who inflict
injustice or unhappiness.

Mary McLeod Bethune

You can only keep a person in the gutter
by getting in the gutter yourself.

Marjory Stoneman Douglas

Enemies must be forgiven.

Mary McLeod Bethune

A man blessed with a good mamma and
a good wife has no right to complain
about anything else.

Claude Pepper

Youthful friendships are among
the greatest things in life.

John Dos Passos

Giving is receiving.

Wally "Famous" Amos

8

Success and Failure

With the possible exception of Texas, no state in the union has weathered more economic storms than Florida. The land of sun and fun has seen its share of booms and busts. Along the way, many fortunes have been made — and lost.

The builders of Florida learned an important lesson: failure is never permanent unless we make it so. Armed with this wisdom, courageous men and women persevered through hurricanes, killing frosts and economic collapse. After each setback, Floridians picked themselves up, dusted away the sand, and started over. Snowbird Henry Ford could have been speaking for the entire state when he observed, "Failure is only the opportunity to begin again, more intelligently." That's wisdom. And that's Florida

M an is not made for defeat.

Ernest Hemingway

B efore everything else, getting ready is
the secret of success.

Henry Ford

T he key to success is the will to succeed,
aided by fortuitous circumstances.

Claude Pepper

Success is the
progressive realization
of a worthy goal.

Earl Nightingale

Success does not come
to you. You go to it.

Wally "Famous" Amos

Our greatest weakness lies in giving up.
The most certain way to succeed is
to always try just one more time.

Thomas Edison

When you blunder, blunder forward.

Thomas Edison

I failed my way to success.

Thomas Edison

Show me a thoroughly satisfied man — and
I will show you a failure.

Thomas Edison

Success in Florida requires courage to face
the hardships cheerfully, patience to wait,
and the energy and spirit to look
ahead to the future through
the hard struggle of the present.

Iza Duffus Hardy

What does it take to be the best?
Everything. And everything is up to you.

Emmitt Smith

Don't give up hope, and take advantage
of every opportunity that comes your way.
Success is destined to follow.

Daniel "Chappie" James

You get as many second chances as you want.

Wally "Famous" Amos

Sometimes you don't know how good you are.
Sometimes you'll even surprise yourself.

Howard Schnellenberger

My best friend is the one
who brings out the best in me.

Henry Ford

If you are serious about improvement,
be brutally honest with yourself.

Greg Norman

Learn from everyone. Copy no one.

Don Shula

The great ones break the rules.
The great ones take chances.

Larry King

It's difficult to excel at something
you don't truly enjoy.

Jack Nicklaus

Successful people are influenced by the
desire for pleasing results.
Failures are influenced by the
desire for pleasing activities.

Earl Nightingale

Character is just as important as ability.

Don Shula

Whether you succeed or fail, you have to try. But if you try, you have not failed.

Rocky Aoki

Don't look down on "failure." I have learned many fascinating things by my failures, things which are as interesting as the successes.

David Fairchild

The only person who could be called a failure is the person who tries to succeed at nothing.

Earl Nightingale

Focus on remedies, not faults.

Jack Nicklaus

Of course there have been successes along
the line, but it has been the anticipation
that has filled my life with pleasure.

David Fairchild

Let the laughter of your successes rise
above the whimpers of your disappointments.

Jesse Earl Bowden

Success is only safe when it comes slowly,
and even then, it is not entirely so.

James Weldon Johnson

Setting goals is an art. A good goal should
be lofty enough to inspire hard work,
yet realistic enough to provide hope.

Greg Norman

I have always been contented,
but I have never been satisfied.

Henry Flagler

Leisure is not success. Successful people
do not have much time for leisure, and
busy people are happy people.

J. E. Davis

The secret of my success? Concentration.

Chris Evert

My formula for success is simple:
practice and concentration — then more
practice and more concentration.

Babe Didrikson Zaharias

No prize changes a man.

Isaac Bashevis Singer, Nobel Prize Winner

Win graciously.

Arnold Palmer

Be gracious in defeat as well as victory and keep success in perspective.

Chris Evert

9

Work

Who was Thomas Edison? He was an inventor, an entrepreneur, a philosopher, and a visionary. He was also a part-time resident of Fort Meyers.

Edison's genius grew out of his dogged determination and astounding perseverance. He endured hundreds of failures in search of a single, elusive success. But when he succeeded, his inventions changed the world forever.

The life of Thomas Edison is a tribute to hard work. He once remarked, "I am glad the eight-hour day had not been invented when I was a young man. If my life had been made up of eight-hour days, I do not believe I could have accomplished a great deal." Spoken by a bright, hardworking Floridian.

The first rule is that a human being must
have something worthwhile
toward which he is working.

Earl Nightingale

There is no substitute for hard work.

Thomas Edison

Work, unflinching work, is the only road
to success for him who starts life
without the golden key.

Iza Duffus Hardy

Work hard and the rest comes easy.

Nick Bollettieri

Unorganized work, performed without
a definite goal, is like rolling a stone
up a mountain of sand.

J. C. Penney

Nothing is particularly hard if you
divide it into small jobs.

Henry Ford

If you refuse to work as hard as you can
to achieve your goal, you're cheating yourself,
whether it's in athletics or in life.

Don Shula

Whatever your job, take pride in hard work.

Idella Parker

Pop didn't teach me golf.
　　　He taught me discipline.

Arnold Palmer

The secret of success? The answer is
　　　summed up in two words: hard work.

J. C. Penney

Genius is one percent inspiration and
　　　ninety-nine percent perspiration.

Thomas Edison

One is not unique in being obliged to toil
and struggle and suffer. This is the simplest
of facts and the most difficult to accept.
Marjorie Kinnan Rawlings

SFN is a worse drug than crack!
SFN, "Something for Nothing," is behind
the breakdown of law and order
and a lot of unhappiness.
J. E. Davis

A lot of people do not recognize
opportunity because it usually goes around
wearing overalls and looking like hard work.
Thomas Edison

Whatever your goal in life, try to do it to
the best of your ability but stay happy.
Wherever you set your sights, don't get
discouraged, and be proud every day that
you are able to work in that direction.

Chris Evert

Match your strategy to your skills.

Arnold Palmer

You'd be surprised how many shortcomings
you can overcome by hustle.

Pete Rose

Everything comes to him who hustles
while he waits.

Thomas Edison

The best place to make a fresh start
after retirement, in our opinion, is Florida.

George and Jane Dusenbury

Luck and laziness make
a pair that never pulled
a load up the hill.

J. C. Penney

10

Adversity

Miami Banker Ed Romfh was fond of saying, "The higher you get, the harder you fall." The same could be said for the high-flying state of Florida. Florida's natural treasures are legion, but mother nature periodically strikes back with a vengeance. And Florida's economic blessings are almost too numerous to count, but periods of explosive growth still lead to times of retrenchment.

Floridians know about adversity. It's the Cuban immigrant making a new life in Miami. It's the family rebuilding after the hurricane. It's the farmer on the frosty night or the captain on the stormy sea. No matter how lovely the surroundings, there must still be, from time to time, trouble in paradise. Here's how Floridians respond.

Expect to lose sometimes, but a loss can be
a stepping stone to victory if used properly.
Jake Gaither

If I'm a good football coach, it's because of
my mistakes. I try to learn from them.
Steve Spurrier

Through the dark days, I was being led
to the development of the talents I loved,
and which have brought
so much enjoyment to us all.
John James Audubon

When you get hurt, use it.
Ernest Hemingway

You may not realize it when it happens,
but a kick in the teeth can be the
best thing in the world for you.

Walt Disney

Don't look forward to the day when you
stop suffering. Because when it comes,
you'll know that you're dead.

Tennessee Williams

The more problems you have,
the more alive you are. I feel most alive
when I'm solving problems.

Bill Peterson

The truest examination of strength
is found in times of adversity.

Bob Graham

As a cure for worry,
      work is better than whiskey.

Thomas Edison

To achieve contentment under adverse
      circumstances requires first
      an adjustment within oneself.

Marjorie Kinnan Rawlings

When I can't handle events,
      I let them handle themselves.

Henry Ford

Concentration is a fine antidote to anxiety.

Jack Nicklaus

Make the total effort,
even when the odds are against you.

Arnold Palmer

One man with courage is a majority.

Andrew Jackson

Y̲ou can overcome any obstacle
in this country. It may just be a little harder
for you than for someone else.

Ray Charles

I̲ don't dwell on bad shots, bad rounds, or
bad tournaments. I don't play in the past — I
play in the present.

Raymond Floyd

I̲f you can react the same way to winning and
losing, that's a big accomplishment.

Chris Evert

Obstacles are what you see when you take your eye off your goal.

Wally "Famous" Amos

It's always too soon to quit.

Steve Spurrier

When something angers you,
you're face to face with opportunity.

Earl Nightingale

The way to improve is to keep trying
through the down times. Keep trying and
keep banging on the door until it opens.

Nick Bollettieri

The most rewarding things in life are often
the things that look like they can't be done.

Arnold Palmer

They may chain our hands and chain our feet,
but the red man's heart will always be free.

Cooacoochee

I would never have amounted to anything
if it were not for adversity.

J. C. Penney

11

The Developers

Florida, more than any other state, is the creation of promoters and developers. From Ponce de León to Flagler and Disney, ebullient entrepreneurs have built the Sunshine State from the beach up. These men and women carved modern cities out of the subtropical wilds — for better or for worse, they made Florida what it is today.

In 1565, author Richard Hakluyt engaged in one of the earliest examples of promotional hyperbole: "The commodities of this land are more than are yet known to any man.... They have apothecary herbs, trees, roots, and gummes great store.... Gold and silver they want not. Of unicorns they have many."

Although sales techniques have become more sophisticated in the intervening centuries, the selling of Florida continues. Anybody need a good unicorn?

The Developers

 A settler in Florida — whether he comes as a
capitalist, as a farmer, or as a laborer — can
live with more ease and personal comfort, can
live more cheaply, can enjoy more genuine
luxuries, can obtain a greater income from a
smaller investment and by less labor, than in
any other accessible portion of North America.

George M. Barbour, 1896

 Industry wants to go where people want to go.
That's Florida.

LeRoy Collins

 Friend Flagler, if you want to find Tampa,
just follow the crowd.

Henry Plant, Spoken to Henry Flagler

No man is smart enough to figure out the
future in great detail, but in Florida, that
is not a hard job. We know what we have.
Moreover, the world knows it.

Peter O. Knight

I want to see things grow.
I want to build things. I like steam shovels
at work. I want to get things done.

Carl Fisher

Florida is all right. I find everything here
that first sold me on the state, and
I know of no reason to change
the opinion I have always held.

Barron Collier
Remarks During a Downturn in the Economy

When I began, I was 23 and full of confidence.
Like any successful businessman today,
I never thought that much about the problems
I faced. I just knew what I wanted to do,
and I went out and did it.

Jim Walter

Restlessness and discontent
are the first necessities of progress.

Thomas Edison

Get a good idea and stay with it. Dog it, and
work at it until it's done, and done right.

Walt Disney

In the Florida building industry,
things change fast.

Frank Mackle, Jr.

How long the boom will last is another
question. One man's guess is as good as
another's. This man's guess is one more year.

George M. Barbour

He made this prediction in 1926.
The land boom went bust one year later.

We are going right ahead with our program
as originally planned. We have not been
affected by the boom, so we are not
suffering from its collapse.

Barron Collier, 1927

Miami will never be more than
  a fishing village for my hotel guests.

Henry Flagler

My dream is to see this wilderness
  turned into prosperous country.

Julia Tuttle, "The Mother of Miami"

Florida is particularly adapted to the needs
  of people who can afford two houses,
  and want a refuge from the drain
  that winter makes on the health.

Harriet Beecher Stowe, 1873

Florida has become a winter playground
  for half a continent.

Federal Writer's Project, 1939

Florida: Where the Gates of Death Are Farther Removed Than From Any Other State

Claim Made By The Flagler Land Companies

Always remember that this whole thing was started by a mouse.

Walt Disney

12

Nature

Mother Nature has favorite children, and Florida is one. The land of Ponce de León and Menéndez is favored by climate and geography, so favored in fact that much of the world seems intent on moving there. With staggering growth comes the need for thoughtful conservation. In recent years, thanks to naturalists like Marjory Stoneman Douglas, citizens have become increasingly aware that natural systems can be fragile. Communities are now seeking a sensible balance between the needs of commerce and the ecological needs of the region. And that's only fair. After all, look at the nice things that Mother Nature has done for Florida.

A warm sunny Florida morning can bring on something like a cosmic feeling of happiness.

David Fairchild

The beauty of the morning is one of the most
rewarding things about South Florida's
late spring and early summer.

Ernest Lyons

A warm climate promises aid
where medicines are utterly ineffectual.

Daniel Garrison Brinton, 1869

The most equitable climate of the United
States is on the south-eastern coast of Florida.

Daniel Garrison Brinton

No state is under greater pressure from all
the forces that place demands upon the land,
water, and life. The United States
begins and ends in Florida.

Raymond F. Dasmann

The future lies in the strength with which
man can set his powers of creation
against his impulses for destruction.
Perhaps this is the unending frontier.

Marjory Stoneman Douglas

It seems to me that the earth may
be borrowed but not bought. It may
be used but not owned. We are tenants,
not possessors, lovers and not masters.

Marjorie Kinnan Rawlings

Quiet places should be enjoyed.
Save the quiet places first.

Ernest Lyons

Once in a while in Florida, Nature,
like a grandmother in a fret, comes down
on you with a most unexpected snub.
You have a cold spell — an actual frost.

Harriet Beecher Stowe

Florida, perhaps more favored by nature
than any other state, has been poorly treated by
nature's twin gangsters, storms and hurricanes.

Fuller Warren

If the freeze or a hurricane cleans out
your groves, you got to take it in stride.
That's just the way the monkey hangs.

Ben Hill Griffin, Jr.

The ocean does not give up easily
her secrets or her animals. Only by diligently
searching will you learn where creatures
spawn, what they eat, and where they hide.

Jack Rudloe

Mangroves: there is something
primeval about them.

Jack Rudloe

The fisherman loves to row out in the
stillness of the mists of the morning when
the lake is like polished black glass.

Ernest Lyons

There are over six hundred species of fish
found in the fresh and saltwaters of Florida.
Florida fishing is still the best in the nation.

T. N. Anderson

Florida Wisdom

Never give up listening
to the sounds of birds.

John James Audubon

There is nothing to compete with Florida oranges but Florida oranges.

Henry Flagler

13

Business Advice

Flowers aren't the only things that blossom in Florida. Capitalism also blooms. From Key West to Pensacola, industrious men and women continue the entrepreneurial traditions of Henry Flagler, Carl Fisher, and Julia Tuttle.

The following ideas comprise a brief primer on the business of business — Florida style.

Golden rule principles are just as necessary for operating a business profitably as are trucks, typewriters, or twine.

J. C. Penney

Florida Wisdom

These are really good times,
   but only a few people know it.

Henry Ford

First, run a tight ship. Second, don't expand
   for the sake of expanding. Finally, always
   believe in quality and service.

Jorge Mas Canosa, Sr.

Overperform. Do more for them than you
   say you're going to do.

Wayne Huizenga

It pays to be liberal in the conduct of business.

Bion H. Barnett, His Favorite Saying

Who is your boss? You have only one.
   The customer.

Earl Nightingale

My philosophy of running a grocery store?
Give the lady what she wants!

George Jenkins, Founder of Publix

If something works, try it on a bigger scale.

Al Neuharth

There is a philosophy of boldness — to take
advantage of every tiny opening
toward victory.

Arnold Palmer

You need to stay close to the action because
you never know what's going to happen.

Ben Hill Griffin, Jr.

If you're selling sports, or about anything
   else for that matter, it should be fun.
      You've got to have a good time.

Pat Williams

If you want to have fun with a business,
   you've got to make money. It's that simple.

Jim Ryder

My business plan? Make money
         and have fun.

Jimmy Buffett

My business means more to me than money.

John Ringling

I prefer "cash flow" to "net earnings."

Ira Koger

I don't have an MBA or anything.
I guess I'm like the old fellow who said if
something costs $1 and you can sell it for $2,
you can make 1% and do pretty well.

Ron Rice, Founder of Hawaiian Tropic

Without the capital required,
one cannot make things happen.

J. E. Davis

I never had any goals. My long-range plan
is simple: stay in business this year.

Ben Hill Griffin, Jr., Citrus Barron

Florida Wisdom

Negotiation is like a chess game.
Sometimes it's your move — sometimes
it's theirs.

A. L. Ellis

First, look where you have an advantage.
Then build on that advantage.

Lawton Chiles

Success is not the result of making money.
Making money is the result of success.

Earl Nightingale

Never rationalize a bad deal.

John D. MacDonald

Never make speculative investments.

Bion H. Barnett

Speculate with your dollars and risk only
to the extent of a good night's rest.
But remember — no risk — no big rewards!

J. E. Davis

Debt, once it gets out of hand, becomes
self-perpetuating. You only end up
borrowing more and more.

Larry King

There's a great similarity between debt and
liquor. Either can be used beneficially,
or either can destroy you.

Ed Ball

I attribute modern successes to one thing:
not luck, not clairvoyance,
not even an intimate knowledge
of a subject, but the ability
to accumulate and handle capital.

J. E. Davis

Discontent is the first necessity of progress.

Thomas Edison

Confusion to the enemy.

Ed Ball's Favorite Toast

It is not the employer who pays wages.
He only handles the money.
It is the product that pays the wages.

Henry Ford

You can learn a million
dollars worth of lessons
from a tough competitor.

"Big Daddy" Don Garlits

The surest way for an executive to kill
himself is to refuse to learn how, and when,
and to whom to delegate.

J. C. Penney

The secret to my success? Find people
who do my job better than I do.

Jack Knight

The first thing I learned in business is this:
find dependable people.

Jimmy Buffett

Focus not on the commotion around you, but on the opportunity ahead of you.

Arnold Palmer

Florida is a businessman's dream.

LeRoy Collins

14

Observations on Spring Training, a Good Night's Sleep, and Other Simple Pleasures of Life

We conclude with an assortment of thoughts on an assortment of subjects.

Whatever it takes, work out a schedule
that permits a full night's sleep.

J. E. Davis

Living successfully is a matter of forming
the right habits.

Earl Nightingale

Not the school, nor the teachers,
but the student is the preponderant
factor in education.

James Weldon Johnson

When we disagree, we learn.

Isaac Bashevis Singer

God is looking for the same thing in each
of us: faith, trust, and commitment.

Bobby Bowden

As human beings, we were born to improvise.

Butterfly McQueen

To be good at anything,
you must be a nonconformist.

Earl Nightingale

Recipe for greatness: To bear up under loss;
to fight the bitterness of defeat;
to be victor over anger;
to smile when tears are close;
to resist evil men and base instincts;
to hate hate and love love;
to look up with unquenchable faith.
That is what any man can do to be great.

Zane Grey

The three great essentials to achieve
anything worthwhile are, first, hard work;
second, stick-to-itiveness;
third, common sense.

Thomas Edison

No man has the right to leave the world no better than he found it.

Edward Bok

We need above all, I think,
a certain remoteness from urban confusion.

Marjorie Kinnan Rawlings

When you talk about plants
you are tranquil, for you know you are
not gossiping or criticizing others.

David Fairchild

The best thinking has been done in solitude.
The worst has been done in turmoil.

Thomas Edison

Late in life there has come to me
an appreciation of the importance of the
education of the senses. My love of the
tropics and southern Florida is directly
related to my sensory education.

David Fairchild

Millions come to Florida — and never see it.
Take the by-ways, drop into quiet little towns
where neon does not yet hide the stars,
visit the Suwanee and the upper St. Johns,
cruise up the St. Lucie.
Be able to say: "We saw the real Florida."

Ernest Lyons

When I was young, my dad whupped
me into line. Thank God he did.

Shaquille O'Neal

Invest in a human soul. Who knows?
It might be a diamond in the rough.

Mary McLeod Bethune

If more politicians were thinking about
the next generation instead of the
next election, it would be better for
the United States and for the world.

Claude Pepper

Don't try to be someone you're not.
They tried to make me into the mold of Babe
Ruth, but I didn't want to fit anyone's mold.

Roger Maris

The penalty of deception is the agony of
an uneasy conscience, and that's far
too great a price to pay for anything.

Edward Bok

Courage is grace under pressure.

Ernest Hemingway

Everyone should make two fortunes:
one to save for old age, the other to blow.
Jackie Gleason

I keep healthy by staying away from doctors.
Ed Ball, who lived to be 93 years old

Fools fall in where angels fear to tread.
Bill Peterson

The serving of good food is one certain way
of pleasing everybody.

Marjorie Kinnan Rawlings

The Grapefruit League is one of the lighter
pleasures of Florida.

Fuller Warren

Working with the land is the most
rewarding of all hobbies.

Ernest Lyons

I have learned a great deal from
listening carefully. Most people never listen.
Ernest Hemingway

A bore is somebody — you ask him
how he is and he tells you.
John D. MacDonald

There's nothing funnier
than the human animal.
Walt Disney

There's a time for departure even
when there's no certain place to go.
Tennessee Williams

And away we go.

Jackie Gleason

As your travel through
life, brother,
Whatever be your goal,
Keep your eye upon
the donut,
And not upon the hole.

Motto of the Downy Flake Donut Company

Orlando, 1935

The best treasures
are yet to be found.

Mel Fisher

Sources

About the Author

Criswell Freeman was born in Orlando. Today, he is a Doctor of Clinical Psychology living in Nashville, Tennessee. Dr. Freeman is the author of *When Life Throws You a Curveball, Hit It* and *The Wisdom Series* from WALNUT GROVE PRESS. In his spare time, he is a published country music songwriter.

The Wisdom Series
by Dr. Criswell Freeman

The Book of All American Wisdom
ISBN 0-9640955-2-1

The Book of Southern Wisdom
ISBN 0-9640955-3-X

The Book of Country Music Wisdom
ISBN 0-9640955-1-3

The Golfer's Book of Wisdom
ISBN 0-9640955-6-4

The Wisdom of Southern Football
ISBN 0-9640955-7-2

The Book of Texas Wisdom
ISBN 0-9640955-8-0

The Book of Florida Wisdom
ISBN 0-9640955-9-9

Wisdom Books are available through
booksellers everywhere. For information about
a retailer near you, call 1-800-256-8584.